PSYCHIC COLD READING
FORBIDDEN WISDOM

TIPS AND TRICKS FOR PSYCHICS, MEDIUMS AND MENTALISTS

DR TERRY WESTON

First published in Great Britain by Swordworks Books

ISBN 978-1-906512-51-4

Printed and bound in the UK & US

A catalogue record of this book is available from the British Library

Cover design by Swordworks Books

PSYCHIC COLD READING
FORBIDDEN WISDOM

CONTENTS

ABOUT COLDREADING   7

FORTUNE TELLING BY CARDS   15

PSEUDO-PALMISTY   23

PSEUDO-GRAPHOLOGY   27

PSEUDO-ASTROLOGY   31

THE WORLD OF DREAMS   35

FORTUNE TELLING BY COINS   39

PSEUDO-NUMEROLOGY   47

SCRIBBLE-OLOGY   51

THE PSYCHIC SYSTEM   55

ADDENDA   61

GLOSSARY OF TERMS   65

ABOUT COLDREADING

Cold Reading is the term of art used by psychics, mediums and magicians to describe the practical use of the Barnum Effect in the give-and-take of an interview situation. Though interest in the technique by professional psychologists dates from the late 1940s, it has long been put to profitable use by fortune tellers, clairvoyants, tarot card readers, astrologers, tea leaf readers, spirit mediums and others who wish to convey the impression that they possess paranormal insight into the client's personality, current life situation or future.

Some paranormal practitioners understand full well the nature and character of the cold reading technique, and the very best work on this subject produced by professional psychologists has been carried out by scholars such as Marks and Hyman who have an independent interest in conjuring. One professional magician who has written eloquently of cold reading is William W. Larsen, Sr. Larsen never claimed in his writings - published privately in the 1930s and 1940s and distributed only for use by professional conjurers - that he possessed any paranormal abilities.

His standard cold reading description is his so-called Life Span Reading, which can be used "straight or with a crystal ball" or can be "given while seemingly reading the subject's palm, laying out the cards, toying with numbers or gazing at tea leaves in a cup".

Many in the audience find the messages highly meaningful, proof that some sort of paranormal powers are being employed. The statements are memorised spiel, delivered according to a code from the assistant to identify the sex and age of each subject:

- "a young lady" means a female 20-30
- "a lady" means 30-55
- "a very nice lady" means 55 and over
- the same three groups for men

From these six crude categories, the appropriate cold reading can be delivered.

Larsen explained to his magician readers that the procedure works so well because the cold reading you will give, to say fifty people, is one that will generally fit any person within the group. Should you fail with one of the fifty, you are still a psychic wonder to the forty nine other people.

The great nineteenth century circus entrepreneur Phineas Taylor Barnum said that "there is a sucker born every minute", or so people claim. There is no record that he ever made such a remark, although Barnum did claim that his success depended on providing in his shows "a little something for everybody". His recipe for success is relevant to understanding the persistent tendency for people to embrace fake personality descriptions as uniquely their own.

The so called Barnum Effect among psychologists dates from Forer's classic experiment in which a group of thirty nine undergraduate psychology students were given the Diagnostic Interest Blank. A week later every student was provided with the same personality description, but was led to believe that each description was uniquely different, having been derived from the test results.

Forer's initial concern was with personality theory and assessment, and the relevance of this effect to understanding "psychic" and apparently paranormal effects was not to begin with widely recognised. As late as 1962 psychologists were calling for the term "Barnum Effect" to be restricted to test-derived clinical personality descriptions of patients which are so general (and trivial) that they apply to everybody.

But the fact that Forer had obtained his generalised personality description not from standard texts in personality theory but from a news stand astrology book which indicated that the Barnum Effect might be significant in contexts far beyond the clinical.

Parts of Forer's phraseology "sexual adjustment" might be effectively put in more modern language, and there are current preoccupations which could be used to make the description even more immediately appealing to contemporary readers.

But this is a description designed to be given to young people of both sexes, and it is remarkable how well it wears after almost forty years.

Slight variations on the original Forer description have been used in numerous studies in the 1950s, 60s and 70s, all in one form or another replicating the remarkable susceptibility of subjects to the Barnum Effect. There has been less agreement on exactly why the Barnum Effect works as well as it does.

The most charitable interpretation would be to say that

Barnum descriptions are simply true of most people: that in endorsing the applicability of Barnum descriptions subjects simply recognise facts. But this account of the situation hardly captures the point of essential interest in Barnum descriptions.

If the consistent endorsement by subjects of Barnum descriptions were merely a matter of recognising their nearly universal applicability, subjects would not then be so prone to treat such descriptions as uniquely describing their own idiosyncrasies.

Subjects, from Forer's original experiment to the present time, would then presumably be more willing to term such descriptions "average" in applying to their own personalities.

Two researchers had bogus student astrologers prepare horoscopes, which were actually uniform Barnum descriptions, for a group of subjects.

The horoscopes were to be rated by the subjects on a 5 point scale:

1. very poor
2. poor
3. average
4. good
5. excellent

Some of the subjects gave the astrologer no birth information at all, members of a second group were required to provide their month of birth, while a third group gave the exact year, month, and day of birth. When asked how closely the horoscope resembled their own personalities, the three groups of students differed significantly.

Those who had given no birth information found the Barnum

description on average to rate 3.58, those the month of birth 3.76, while for those who had revealed their exact date of birth the approval average shot up to 4.38.

Another experiment which revealed the importance of the perceived source of the description was carried out by Silverman.

He presented subjects who possessed a minimal familiarity with astrology with twelve sun-sign personality descriptions.

When the personality descriptions were presented merely numbered, subjects had no tendency to choose the one derived from their own sun sign more often than chance would dictate. But when the descriptions were correctly labelled according to the astrological sign, there was a marked tendency for subjects to choose their own sign.

While the experiments show quite conclusively that a Barnum description is more striking when it is believed to be derived from a credible source, they also indicate that people are often likely to be impressed by Barnum descriptions which involve some sort of arcane "mumbo-jumbo". While a Barnum description may gain in believability when it is thought to be derived from a "credible" source, such as a professional psychologist, it may have even more charm for a subject if it is thought to be derived from a mystical or "incredible" source, such as the lines on the palm of the hand, or the order of cards from a Tarot deck.

Much depends on the prior beliefs and predispositions the subject brings to their encounter with the description. One of Snyder's studies showed that projective tests produced greater belief in a Barnum description than either interview by a psychologist or (with the lowest belief rating of all) objective tests. The reason given by Snyder for the differential is that projective tests and to a lesser degree diagnostic interviews, are surrounded by an air of mystery.

But there is a further point at stake. A projective test would seem to the subject to involve a more creative manifestation of self than ticking off letters on a multiple-choice objective test. Though from a professional viewpoint the results of any projective test may be utterly conventional and typical for a group of subjects, to the naive subject the test will very likely be thought of as something which yields a unique product of their creative personality. This, compounded by the fact that the interpretation of the test is presumably a subtle and mysterious process, leaves the subject in most cases more than willing to validate the result if it is to their liking.

Other investigators have concluded that subjects are more inclined to accept positive than negative Barnum statements about themselves. It is important to understand exactly what negative words form part of a Barnum description, and exactly how they are used in the general context of the descriptions in order to evaluate any particular study. The original Forer description was not unqualifiedly flattering in content, and reason would suggest that pure flattery would not necessarily be the best way to enhance the appeal of a Barnum description.

It is not simply a matter of undesirable descriptions being tolerated if they are presented in a generally flattering context. They can even add to the credibility of a Barnum description by giving it a greater sense of realism than mere flattery could have. Subjects in general are not unwilling to admit that they have problems and faults. The most successful Barnum description is often one which allows this, but does so by generally telling the subject that in the final analysis they are really a splendid person.

Though this is a point of dispute among professional psychologists, it is well recognised in practice by paranormal "professionals" who make use of the Barnum Effect in peddling their horoscopes and psychic readings. But even where there are negative or undesirable elements in a Barnum description, subjects have in any event a strong tendency to notice and remember only a percentage of available items. Confirmations are remembered, often quite vividly, whereas less plausible aspects of the description are paid less attention. Since the point of a Barnum description is that it be general enough to apply to almost anyone, the subject will be hard pressed to identify any item in the description which is plainly wrong.

Where a group of people receive the same Barnum description, it will be read differently by everyone. Each will concentrate on those aspects of the description which seem best to fit a prior self-image. The Barnum description is supposed to fit a human personality. It is not surprising that something as uncertain and complex as the human personality should be subject to a large number of equally plausible descriptions.

Young people in particular, the most frequent subjects of psychologists' studies of the Barnum Effect, often have a sense of the qualities of self which they share with others or which distinguish them as individuals. They easily succumb to the charms of a well devised Barnum description. The uncertainty felt by many people, young or old, about their own personalities also explains the possibly self-fulfilling character of horoscopes.

So where does that leave us with respect to cold reading? What we are trying to show is that cold reading is the art, or science perhaps, of using a variety of generalisations, tailoring them to fit the subject, honing them by means of feedback from the subject themselves, so as to arrive at a reading that is uncannily accurate. Yet the reading has been arrived at by means of information that was either generalised or specific following the sitter's feedback.   This is true for mediums, psychics, clairvoyants, Tarot readers and many other systems of fortune telling and the imparting of so called secret knowledge.

The next section is the start of the "quick and dirty" cold reading techniques that this book is all about. Cold reading is not especially hard to understand, but often difficult to practice when you are put on the spot. What we have done is collected together the "Forbidden Knowledge" and a collection of tried and tested techniques for you to learn and put into practice to help make cold reading work for you.

Good luck!

FORTUNE TELLING BY CARDS

These are three unusual methods for telling fortunes with cards in an entertaining and mystifying way using simple sleights familiar to magicians.

THE TRIPLE TURNOVER

Ask the person whose fortune is to be told to shuffle the deck and cut it into three packs on the table. Pick up one pile at a time and drop it on the table. Each time a card seems to jump out of the pack and turn face-up on the top and from these you tell the person's fortune by giving the meaning of each card.

The sleight employed is the old familiar "push-over". Pick up each pile of cards in turn and with your left hand transfer it to your right hand, the left thumb pushes the top card, off side about half an inch. This is covered by the right hand, which grasps the pile front above; fingers being at forward end and thumb at rear of packet. Now drop the pile on table from a height of twelve to eighteen inches and the offset card will turn over in mid-air automatically, landing face up on the packet.

The effect is mysterious and surprising. It looks as if a card actually jumped out. You can attribute any meaning you wish to that card, as long as it sounds good.

It is good to interpret these three face-up "fortune cards" as Past, Present and Future.

Examples:

Jack of Diamonds -
"In your youth you were deeply impressed by a young man. He spent money on you, entertained you, and influenced your thoughts and actions etc."

Five of Hearts –
"You are about to receive unexpected news concerning a dear friend. Someone you have not seen for a long while etc."

Three of Spades
"In the immediate future I see a long journey for you on matters which will bring you prominently before the public etc."

OUT OF THE HAT

This is a novel method and the principle is not generally known to the public. Have a person shuffle the cards. Take the deck and place it in a hat, snap on bottom of hat, and some cards jump out and flutter to the floor. These cards you use to tell the fortune.

Use a soft felt hat for this, creasing it lengthwise through the centre of the crown, thus forming two compartments. As you place the deck in the hat separate a few cards and allow these to go on one side of the ridge, while the rest of the deck is on the other.

Left hand supporting the hat gives a little squeeze so that the loose cards rest nicely upright in their separate section. The hat may be shaken a bit, as if to mix the cards (but it doesn't).

Now with right fingers and thumb snap sharply on the crown of the hat directly beneath the spot where the few cards are, which will cause them to jump out of the hat and flutter down. Give the meaning of these cards as the person's fortune, as previously described. Then tip out all the cards from the hat on table. You will find this very effective . . . and surprising, too.

THE MENTAL WONDER

An astounding effect, if well presented. The principle is so simple and bold, it often fools magicians. In effect, the person cuts a shuffled deck and while your back is turned, deals off a few cards face down on the table. He does not look at them YET, but you begin to tell your impressions about certain cards affecting his life and future. At conclusion, he looks at the cards and finds them to be the ones you gave a reading from.

The secret is simple, but clever. While handling the deck beforehand secretly note the four cards on top of deck then false shuffle to retain them, and request the person to cut. As he sets the cut-off portion aside, or on the palm of your hand, you immediately place the under portion on top . . . but, you place it cross-wise. This is known as x-ing the cut. Do this boldly, without hesitation, and immediately misdirect attention by emphasising that "You cut anywhere. I did not influence you etc."

Tell the party to remove the upper portion and from where they cut deal off about four cards face-down on table. By motion indicate what he is to do. As soon as you see they are following instructions correctly, turn your back (or step out of the room, but at speaking distance). Now the cards on table will be the four cards secretly noted, so that it becomes a simple matter to tell the person that certain cards influence your life etc. Weave in the names and meanings of the known cards and, for the climax, have him turn the cards over. When he finds your clairvoyant impressions are correct, it is always a stunning surprise. Please try this.

In the Simplified Interpretations of the Cards which follows, are the readings for the various cards, which you can learn. However, if you prefer, just give a reading of your own invention . . . it's the effect that counts!

SIMPLIFIED INTERPRETATION OF THE CARDS

It is for use with fortune telling effects.

It is an easy and quick system to learn, once acquired will never be forgotten.

You need to commit to memory a list of thirteen events for the various card values. These are applied to the Sphere of Action as indicated by the four suits. Therefore every card has a distinct and different meaning, these being variations and modifications of the original thirteen.

The Suits - Indicate the Sphere of Action

- Hearts - home life (the family, relations, and loved ones)
- Diamonds - business (means of livelihood, finances etc.)

- Clubs - social life (friends, recreation, hobbies, etc.)
- Spades - civic life (the public, law, authorities, rivals)

The Values - Indicate Events of Importance

- King - a man influencing you (association indicated by the suit)
- Queen - a woman influencing you (association indicated by the suit)
- Jack - young person or child (association indicated by the suit)
- Ten - a gain of money (source indicated by the suit)
- Nine - a loss of money (source indicated by the suit)
- Eight - opposition, quarrels, reverses (indicated by the suit)
- Seven - success, fame, notoriety (indicated by the suit)
- Six - a change, chance, investment, gamble (modify by the suit)
- Five - unexpected news (regarding what, indicated by the suit)
- Four - health (by suit, H - robust, D - fair, C - an accident, S - illness)
- Three - a long journey (on matters indicated by the suit)
- Two - short trip/s (on matters indicated by the suit)
- Ace - partnership or agreement (by suit, H - marriage, D - business,
- C - engagement, S - legal)
- Red Cards predominating are favourable, indicate good fortune
- Black Cards predominating are unfavourable, indicate misfortune

HOW TO MEMORISE

For practice, take a shuffled deck and turn one card at a time face-up. Mentally rehearse the event only, indicated by its value and for now disregarding the suit. By the time you have gone through the fifty two cards, you will recognise the thirteen value-meanings instantly.

Then go through the deck more slowly, rehearsing the complete interpretation of each card as shown by the value plus the sphere of action implied by the suit. Thus you build up a complete set of fifty two definitions, although actually memorising only thirteen. You will soon acquire the method of correlating the meanings of suit and value, and be able to give an interesting reading by cards.

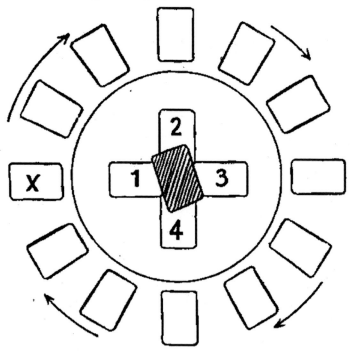

THE MYSTIC CIRCLE

Have the subject shuffle the cards and cut them three times, then deal out seventeen cards on the table as in diagram, twelve cards around the circle and five in the centre, all face-up except the central one, the Wish Card face down.

This arrangement gives a complete reading from the cradle to the grave. Read the cards around the circle - childhood, youth, maturity, old age.

The four cards within the circle interpret:-
This Year:

• No. 1 to occur within 3 months
• No. 2 within 6 months
• No. 3 within 9 months
• No. 4 within the year

The Wish Card is turned up last.

How to Give an Interesting Reading

Starting at the point marked "x" and reading clockwise, study the meanings of the first three cards, interpreting both value and suit. Give a reading for these either separately or combined, as seems to fit the case. These are happenings, events or influences occurring in the person's childhood. Telling a bit of the past inspires confidence in your ability.

Now study the next group of three cards and the events of the person's youth.

Continuing around into the lower part of the circle the next group of three show the major events of mature life which run into old age, as predicted by the last three cards. This brings you around to the starting point and completes the life reading.

Now study the four face-up cards inside the circle and from these predict events to happen. Finally, turn the centre card face up. This is the Wish Card and reveals the subject uppermost in the person's mind at the moment. If they have previously made a wish this card will indicate the answer:-

- Hearts, certain of fulfilment
- Diamonds, quite likely
- Clubs, uncertain
- Spades, not entirely

REMEMBER!

You tell fortunes for entertainment purposes only. Temper your remarks accordingly. Don't be too pessimistic. Maintain a cheery attitude and an encouraging outlook throughout. Interpret an unfavourable event as, a lesson to be learned, a necessary stepping-stone in the development of character and personality.

You will find it very easy to present an interesting reading, and reap much enjoyment for yourself and others. Despite the fact that this secret system is so simple to you, your friends will see your ability as wonderful. It is surprising how often your predictions will come true, those that do not are invariably forgotten anyway.

You will soon get the knack of it and develop a smooth, confident, and easy- flowing style.

PSEUDO-PALMISTY

Ideal for private and social entertainment. The entertainer is blindfolded for this act. He claims that his fingertips are keener when outside influences are eliminated and the subject is unknown to him. Any spectator is invited to volunteer. The magician passes his fingers over the spectator's palm, feeling the lines and mounts and interpreting their meaning in an interesting personalised analysis, giving intimate details of the past and predictions for the future. Nothing is spoken by the subject and no questions are asked.
This, plus the blindfold, makes the act unique in itself and tremendously impressive.

The secret of the act is that, despite the blindfold, the performer identifies the spectators by their shoes. The reading is a combination of:-

- previous observation
- advance information
- showmanship

No actual knowledge of palmistry is necessary, though a familiarity with the terminology of the profession is impressive.

Before the demonstration carefully observe the shoes worn by each guest in attendance and gather an impression of the type of person they are.

Note general appearance, age, stature, facial features, expression and disposition. Small details are often the key to character - clothes, hairstyle, jewellery, etc.

In advance pump the host for as much personal information about people as possible:-

- interests
- hobbies
- aspirations
- name of husband, wife or partner
- little details of their life, dates, things expected soon

It is surprising how much can be learned without being obvious. The person's own name and things everybody knows are not important. Minor events with dates, and things they look forward to - reference to friends, relatives and experiences are very impressive.

THE PRESENTATION:

Give a brief talk on palmistry, stressing the fact that the blindfold eliminates all external impressions and allows you to concentrate upon the aspects of the palm as you sense them through the fingertips.

Ask them not to speak, as you will not ask any questions. The conditions which you impose make deception impossible.

Now you are blindfolded say that any person may now come up and place their palm beneath your fingertips. The blindfold does not prevent you from looking down alongside the nose and seeing their shoes. Proceed to build up a reading, while running your fingers lightly over the person's palm.

Correlate your interpretations with the lines and mounts of the hand. Besides purely descriptive generalities, weave in as many intimate details as you have been able to glean. When information is inadequate, or memory fails, make use of one of the sure-fire predictions to fill in. The rest is purely showmanship and an impressive delivery.

Study the sample reading and charts. Reading books on palmistry will enable you to talk the subject with authority before and after the act.

The Lines and Mounts of the Hand.

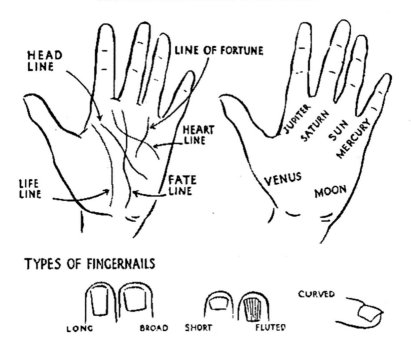

TYPES OF FINGERNAILS

LONG   BROAD   SHORT   FLUTED   CURVED

A SAMPLE READING

From observation and information

This is the hand of a happy type of person, one who loves to laugh and make people happy. The shapes of your fingers indicate an artistic temperament and in your youth you made sacrifices to study art. You have a natural talent for music and play the piano very well. Long nails show excellent taste in clothes and your favourite colour is blue.

The Mount of Mercury shows your love of jewellery and diamonds are your favourite stone. Your Heart Line shows marriage at the age of twenty three very plainly.

You are happily married to a man who loves all kinds of sport and you both enjoy the outdoors.

You have nothing to worry about financially in the future is clearly shown by your Fate Line. You have had your share of trials and troubles, but these are now over.

Your son, Brian, worships his father.

The Mount of Jupiter is prominent, showing popularity with friends and acquaintances.

You may expect, very shortly now, something you have wanted very intensely, maybe a new car.

PSEUDO-GRAPHOLOGY

Handwriting analysis for entertainment. In this act small blank memo pads and pencils are distributed to spectators for them to write, "This is a specimen of my handwriting." and nothing else.

These are then collected in a hat or bowl and placed on the table where the performer is seated.

By candlelight the performer studies each specimen and analyses each one in an uncannily accurate manner, telling the character, abilities, and interests.

The paper is rolled into a ball and given to each person to hold until later. This is repeated as desired. At the finish the performer declares that he will cause spirit writing to appear as proof of his occult powers.

Everyone opens his paper and is amazed to find their initials, nickname, or phone number has appeared as a signature of his own writing.

A very fine mystery act for private parties, as it is a distinctly a different form of entertainment.

Required:-

- a quantity of memo-pads, about 3x5 inches in size
- pencils
- a short, fancy candle holder
- a bottle of invisible ink (lemon juice)
- a new, clean pen

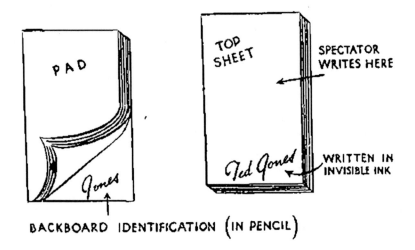

BACKBOARD IDENTIFICATION (IN PENCIL)

PREPARATION

Before the act, consult the host or hostess for a list of names of those present and a bit of information about each. Have each person pointed out to you (secretly, of course) so that you will know them. In private prepare a pad for each one.

Write the person's name on the backing of the pad, as illustrated. Then with invisible ink write person's initials, name or phone number on the lower part of the top sheet of the pad. This dries quickly and cannot be seen. Then arrange the pads in order, either alphabetically or anyway you wish.

When distributing the pads at the start of the act if there is any doubt as to whom that pad belongs to, you can make sure by just lifting the pad a bit, as shown, with the thumb and get a glimpse of the name. This is an added safety feature to be used only if necessary.

PRESENTATION

After a few remarks about the science of graphology and the secrets of character as revealed by hand-writing, distribute the pads and pencils apparently at random (but really to the proper parties).

Tell them to write only the words, "This is a sample of my handwriting".

While this is being done, return to table and light the candle.

Have papers torn off and pads set aside. Specimen sheets are then collected, mixed, and placed on table at one side, while the candle is set directly in front of you.

Take one paper at a time and scrutinise it closely, holding it over the candle to illuminate from below to see details better. The heat from the flame will develop the invisible writing rapidly, but this is hidden from audience by your hands cupped around the paper.

You therefore know the writer of that particular specimen and proceed to give a reading from observation and information furnished by the obliging host. Attribute each remark to some characteristic of the writing, i.e., the slant, height, shape, form of the letters and peculiar flourishes typical of the writer.

Eventually, as your delineation becomes more exact, speak directly to the party and get his or her acknowledgement as fitting his case. Then roll the paper into a small ball and hand it to the owner to hold until later. At the end say you will cause spirit-writing to appear as a symbol of your occult powers. Wave your hands mysteriously over the closed fist of each spectator, then have them open the papers. They find a spirit-signature has appeared on each and keep the paper as souvenirs.

The surprise at the finish is a big feature.

A suggestion:
While no actual scientific study is required to put over this act, it is well to know something about graphology in order to talk convincingly about it, before or after performance.

  Books on the subject make interesting reading and are available at public libraries or book shops.

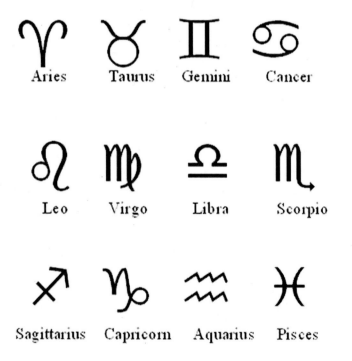

PSEUDO-ASTROLOGY

Three novel methods for telling fortunes, with an astrological theme and a magical twist, each adapted for a special purpose.

PRESENTATION NO. 1 (FOR IMPROMPTU OCCASIONS)

This is a short, snappy version to work right out of the pocket. Have a small pocket notebook, the pages of which are prepared as follows.

On each sheet inscribe the Zodiac sign for the month of the year, i.e. for April, the sign of Aries in invisible ink, lemon juice will do written with a tooth pick. This dries out and cannot be seen until heat is applied, when it materialises black. Make up sheets for all the months, January to December. You can look up the symbols quite easily.

Now with a pencil dot somewhere on the edge of sheet, code them so you will know what sheet to use for January, February, March, etc.

To Present:

Inquire the birthday, month and day, of the person, at the same time taking the notebook from your pocket. Tear out a sheet for that month, which appears to be unprepared and is to be used to write notations on.

Proceed to tell about the planetary influences under the Zodiac sign of Leo (for example) in August, dominated by the sun, lucky stone is the ruby, fortunate colour red, etc.

As you talk, make pencil notations on the paper which you are going to give the person as a souvenir.

And "To prove my psychic powers, I shall cause a mystical symbol of your birth month to appear."

So saying, light a match and hold paper over the flame, when the person will see his Zodiac sign materialise visibly and almost instantly.

An excellent surprise climax, and a lucky charm for the person to carry as a souvenir, (you tell them).

No extensive knowledge of astrology is necessary in any of these presentations, but a little background on the subject is helpful.

PRESENTATION NO. 2

This is a more subtle method. You don't ask them to name their birth month, but obtain this information secretly. Therefore, you receive more credit for psychic ability.

Preparation:

Take two small envelopes and a card to fit. One envelope is faked by cutting an oval shaped hole in its face. This is in a pocket to start, and is used as follows:-

Hand unprepared envelope containing blank card to the person. Have him remove the card and with pencil you inscribe an oval on same, with a line lengthwise through the centre. Hand him the pencil and pick up the envelope. Instruct him to write his birth month and day above the line and a subject of interest (i.e., love, business, etc.) below the line.

While he does this, you turn your back. Switch the unprepared envelope for the faked one, which you hold in such way that he doesn't see the open face. Tell him to lay the card face down on the table after he has written. Swing around, envelope in hand, and slide his card face down, unseen by you in the envelope, which is also face down. Naturally, he presumes it to be the same envelope which he first handled. Now, holding same with open-face towards yourself, strike a match and ignite the envelope, the same time noting what he has written.

As the evidence is consumed, begin to tell him about the astrological forces predominating at the time he was born. Take the notebook from your pocket and tear out proper blank(?) page. This is prepared with invisible ink. Proceed along the same lines as in Presentation No.1, for the appearance of his mystic symbol and Zodiac sign.

A variation is to have papers prepared to match size of envelopes, a set of twelve, one for each month. One of these is taken from the pocket, instead of notebook, the paper sealed in envelope having been initialled by the person himself. The symbol will materialise just as well, despite the envelope. Hand this sealed envelope to him at the finish, when he opens it he finds the Zodiac sign appearing mysteriously on his own marked paper.

SMALL PRESENTATION

This is more elaborate, designed for a group of persons, strangers to you.

Required:

> A quantity of small memo pads. Top sheet of each is prepared with invisible ink, a symbol of one of the planets being used since you don't know the Zodiac sign of these persons in advance.
>
> On the table arrange a set-up of a crystal globe set in the centre of the Zodiac Chart for atmosphere.
>
> A lit candle.

Working Method:

Hand out pads and pencils to audience, on which they are to write their birth month and day, any subject of interest and their initials. These are collected in a hat or bowl by assistant and placed before you on table. Taking up one at a time, and using the information from chart as a prompter, deliver an astrological reading for each. As you talk hold each paper over the burning candle and thus bring out the mystic symbol, which they do not see until paper is returned to them by assistant, at conclusion of the reading.

THE WORLD OF DREAMS

Dreams and their meanings have long been a mystical subject, and we now combine these in a distinctly. novel act for drawing-room and social entertainment.

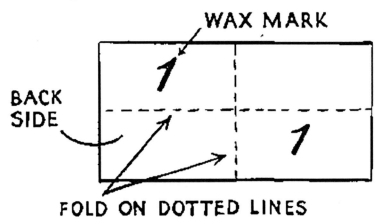

REQUIRED:

A quantity of small blank pads. Take one and lift up the top sheet. Using a small wax birthday candle write the number 1 in two places, on the sheet as illustrated. Do the same with all the pads, numbering them consecutively. The purpose of this is that when the paper is written on and folded twice (with writing inside), a number will be on the outside, though this is invisible.

However, knowing what to look for you will find that, by tipping same in the light, a reflection will be caught of the number so written. By this means you will be able to identify the writer.

Have the prepared pads piled in order. Distribute these in the audience from left to right, handing each person a small pencil. They are to write just one word, something they dreamed about recently and nothing else. Then the papers are to be folded (illustrate by folding one, as per sample), writing inside, of course.

When this has been done, collect same in a hat or deep bowl. Some drop their papers in and sometimes you take their slips and drop them into hat. Remember whose slip this is. Now, on the way back to table, glance down and note the dream word written on the one paper you secretly opened. This gives you the start as will be described; and this paper is left in the hat until last.

Seated at the table, with incense burning on one side and a mystic fire bowl on the other, reach into the hat and pick up any of the folded slip. Hold to forehead and begin to talk about the meaning of dreams about animals (or whatever). Finally talk directly to the person whose slip you know and get his acknowledgment that your impressions of his dream are correct. Meanwhile you have lowered the folded paper before you.

Now, as if to verify, you open the paper and read aloud the

word dog (the word you glimpsed in the hat).

Actually, and unknown to the audience, you read and remember the subject written on the No. 6 paper, which is to be your next interpretation. You are one ahead on information now. Take another folded paper from hat and repeat the operation, getting an impression that someone dreamed about snakes (or whatever you just read) and you direct remarks to the sixth man from left end of row. Each time, after giving the significance, toss paper into fire bowl, where the evidence is consumed. Continue in the same manner throughout, finishing with the opened slip, which you refold before taking it from hat.

The fact that you talk directly to the person and knowing positively who dreamed about so-and-so (although all papers are unsigned and alike, is what fools even those who know the one ahead principle).

The meanings which you give are imaginary. The mystic fire bowl contains alcohol with salt added, which gives a weird, greenish flame.

Very effective atmosphere.

FORTUNE TELLING BY COINS

A novel method for impromptu work at table, or anywhere

Part 1:

Have a person remove ALL the coins they have in their possession, count them secretly and hold same in closed fist as they make the following mental calculations to mine their "fortune by numbers" e.g.

suppose they have	38p
double	76p
double again	£1.52
multiply by five	£7.60

They tell you the final number only and from this you tell their fortune (according to the system given below) such as:-

No.7 - shows that the undertaking you have in mind will be a big success

No.6 - indicates that you are due for a decided change for the better

No.0- predicts a gain of money and popularity for you soon

Part 2:

Now the person is told to drop some of the coins from hand to table, from a height of about twelve inches. As they fall and arrange themselves in some sort of group, you gaze at them (similar to reading leaves in a teacup) and see, or seem to see, a suggestion of some object, animal or thing.

For example a bird, which always means a trip for you etc.

Part 3:

As further proof of your psychic powers, you now unexpectedly name the amount of coins they have in their pocket, correctly!

The subtlety of this lies in the fact that you do not see the coins they have in the beginning...nor at the finish.

The secret is very simple if you know how!

In Part 1 all of the calculations are made by the person mentally, but they do tell you the final figures.

As the last figure is always 0, you consider only the 76. Secretly dividing this by 2 gives you 38p, so you know the amount they have to start. (They don't realise this).

In Part 2, some of the coins are dropped to table, from which you continue to tell their fortune. Secretly noting this amount (i.e. say 24p), you subtract mentally from 38 and thus learn the amount of change remaining in their pocket (i.e.14p). This always works.

The fortune telling idea in the presentation misdirects attention from the basic factor which is mathe-magical.

For your convenience, the following "Meanings of Numbers" are given:-

- No. 1 - contract, engagement or marriage
- No. 2 - short trip
- No. 3 - long journey
- No. 4 - accident
- No. 5 - unexpected news
- No. 6 - change or chance
- No. 7 - success
- No. 8 - opposition, quarrels, reverses
- No. 9 - loss
- No. 0 - gain

FORTUNE TELLING WITH DICE

This is a very mystifying impromptu effect, combining fortune telling - past, present and future. It seems as if a person rolled unprepared dice five times:-

On two of the rolls, they tell you the spots showing, from which you interpret important events in their past life. Then, without asking any further questions, you tell their present fortune, future prospects, lucky number etc. revealing the spots secretly thrown as well as the total of all. This leaves them utterly amazed at your psychic power (?).

The Presentation Routine

Hand out a pair of dice, a pencil and a slip of paper marked with lines and circles as in Fig. 1. Turn your back and tell the person to roll the dice and name the number of spots uppermost (i.e. 8). This you interpret as meaning that in the past you have run into much opposition on things you wanted

41

to do, etc. Tell him to note that figure (8) on top line of paper. "Now look at the total spots on the bottom of the dice...do not tell me, as they signify your lucky number, but write the figure in one of the circles, please."

His paper will now appear as in Fig. 2.

"Please roll the dice again and count the spots on top...do not tell me, as they pertain to the future, but note this in one of the other circles." Then...

"Tell me the number of spots on the bottom of the dice (i.e. 5) ...this means that all your life, the important things have come as a big surprise to you...always unexpected."

His paper will now appear as in Fig. 3, except that the last circle will be blank.

"Now, please make a wish and roll the dice for the last time. Note this number in the remaining circle...and add the total of all, but do not let me see the paper."

As you swing around say that -

"If the number you last threw was odd, you will get your wish...if even, probably not."

This implies that you paid no attention to the last throw. Actually, you mentally add last number, (i.e. 7) to 28, making 35...which you now know is his secret total in this case. At this point, emphasise that –

"You rolled the dice five times, and I have interpreted two of those numbers, which you told me, but I shall now attempt to delve into your future as indicated by those numbers which you have not told me."

Fig. 1.	Fig. 2.	Fig. 3.
Blank paper	After 1st roll	After 2 rolls
_____	8	8
_____	_____	_____
( )	_____	5
( )	(6)	_____
( )	( )	(6)
	( )	(9)
		(7) †
		_____
		35 Total

† (This is the **Final Extra Roll, which you never reveal**)

"Please concentrate on your final total. I get the impression a number 3 is involved, meaning a long journey for you soon. There is the vibration of number 5 present, which indicates that the matter is not now known to you, but will come as unexpected news. Your total 35...is that right?"

"Now, the numbers you have marked in the circles are known only to yourself, yet one of these is your lucky number, which is 6, and you should start all new ventures on the 6th day of the month at the 6th hour...for good luck. And there is another secret number, which you have been keeping from me...Yes...the number 9 always presages a loss of money, very soon...not much this time, and you can just write it off to experience."

The SECRET is based on the fact that on any roll of the dice, top and bottom spots will always total 14, when added together. Note that each roll they tell you one of the numbers, i.e., in this case - 1st roll, top spots total 8, so bottom spots had to be 6; on 2nd roll, they tell you the bottom spots (5) so you know that the top spots were 9 this time. You do not reveal this, however until the very last thing.

Several subtleties in the routine serve to confound those who may think they know:-

1. The numbers are not set down on paper in the same order thrown.
2. At one time they tell you the top spots and another time tell you only the bottom spots. This confuses the subject, but not yourself, as it makes no difference in your mental subtraction from the key-number, 14 ... and you know the other (secret) number immediately.
3. The final number thrown causes the total to be above 28, and to vary...should you repeat the stunt. Also, they don't know that you have secretly noted the top spots on dice at the finish. Later on, in your patter, you mention that "There were three numbers which you did not tell me." (absolutely true)
4. You don't interpret or reveal your knowledge of this last number, but it informs you of the final total by adding same to 28 mentally.

You can use the following Key Words for interpreting the numbers and build up around these or vary as imagination suggests:-

1. - a contract or legal matter
2. - a short trip
3. - a long journey
4. - health or accident
5. - unexpected news

44

6. - a change of some kind
7. - success, publicity, notoriety
8. - opposition, quarrels
9. - a loss
10. - a gain of money
11. - partnership or engagement
12. - investments

PSYCHIC COLD READING FORBIDDEN WISDOM

PSEUDO-NUMEROLOGY

YOUR FORTUNE BY NUMBERS

This is a clever and entertaining method for presenting Numerology, with a surprise revelation as a climax. Requiring no preparation, it is perfect for parties and impromptu occasions whenever the subject of fortune telling arises. Also, because of its simplicity, it is very easy to remember the system.

Presentation and Working Method:

Hand the person a blank piece of paper and a pencil, telling him to write as you will instruct. Step away, so that you do not see their calculations, as per the following example:

Write the Month and Day you were born, in figures

August 3rd	83
Double it	x 2
	166
Double it x 2	
	332
And Multiply by Five	x 5
Lucky Number 1660	

From these figures (1660) you tell the person's fortune.

> "I see that you are about to become a party to an important contract, which will mean a great deal to you (1), and you will also make some change in either your business or your residence which undoubtedly will be for the better (6). Furthermore, I interpret the second 6 to mean that you will take a chance on some new undertaking or investment. And the 0 signifies that this will surely result in a gain of money for you."

(Or, if you prefer, just use your imagination...after all, it is the effect, rather than the method, which counts.)

Now continue your interpretation, as the case and circumstances will suggest, weaving into your remarks the fact that "You were born under the sign of so-and-so ... in August...were you not? And your lucky number is 3, because you were born on that day. If possible, do all your important work and start new ventures on the third day of any month and on the third hour...for luck is with you then."

You are able to reveal this by a simple mental calculation. Disregard the last digit which is always 0. Take the first three (or four) numbers from the total they gave you (i.e. 166) and divide by 2. This will, invariably, inform you the birthday numbers the person originally wrote (83).

The following are my interpretations for:-

The Significance of Numbers

1. - contract, engagement or marriage
2. - short trip
3. - long journey
4. - accident or concerning health
5. - unexpected news
6. - change or chance
7. - success
8. - opposition and reverses
9. - loss of money or friend
10. - gain of money or fame

SCRIBBLE-OLOGY

Lecture Theme:

"With your co-operation, I shall demonstrate something new in the field of psychic science, based on the well known fact that so many people have a habit of scribbling apparently meaningless designs, entirely unrelated to the subject upon which they are thinking or concentrating. You may have noticed some people do this, even while talking on the telephone. The action is entirely unconscious and uncontrolled.

Scientific tests and observations indicate that these automatic writings are a manifestation of the sub-conscious mind and as such do have definite meanings. It is thought that scribbles or doodles disclose the character and hidden abilities of the individual and I shall demonstrate what can be done by a study of this interesting subject...with your own specimens."

(while this is going on, pads and pencils are distributed in the audience)

> "Please take your pencils and, while thinking of any abstract subject, allow yourself to draw or scribble at random. Please don't study any special designs. Genuine scrawls are always unconsciously executed and seldom bear any relation to the subject which your mind is consciously engaged.
> This takes only a moment and, when ready, your papers will be collected.
> Please do not sign or otherwise mark your papers, but mix them on the tray, and bring them to me here at the table."

Demonstration:

The performer takes one specimen at a time, studies it for a moment, makes various measurements and delivers an interesting character study and interpretation of the scrawl. Eventually he becomes so definite that identification of the scrawl is unmistakable and the paper is returned directly to the person who wrote it . . . and is acknowledged by him.

The amount of personal details given in the analysis is uncannily accurate and especially appreciated by audiences.

Secret and Working Method:

You may use blank pads, all the same. The top sheet of each pad is marked beforehand in an invisible manner by writing consecutive numbers in lower left hand corner of each paper using a small birthday candle. Ordinarily this cannot be seen, but by tilting the paper in the light you can catch a reflection, if you know what and where to look for it.

The pads are distributed in a predetermined way, from left to right in audience. So you will know that paper No.

6, for example, belongs to the 6th man in the front row, etc. Thus you instantly identify the writer of each specimen secretly and can give an appropriate analysis. Your remarks are based on impressions from observation of the person. But the sensational features have their origin in little bits of information pumped from the host or a talkative member of the committee beforehand, i.e., hobbies, interests etc. The rest is imagination, a glib tongue, and showmanship.

At the table, for supposed analysis, use a small ruler, a draftsman's guide or a magnifying glass. Such accessories will add a touch of scientific atmosphere to your work.

THE PSYCHIC SYSTEM

The system described may be applied to any type of presentation. Whether you tell fortunes from tea leaves, cards, crystal gazing, astrology, palms or even dropping a handful of sand or matches on the table. These are merely the tools of the trade, the medium of interpretation, a means to an end. A satisfactory reading must touch on the subject of interest to the particular individual.

The following is a carefully planned system of approach to determine the person's interest, the subject they would like to hear about. Once that is discovered, it is easy to give an effective delineation and an encouraging message along that line.

The first, and very important, requisite is an accurate, detailed observation of the person:-

- face
- eyes
- hair

- skin
- hands
- nails
- clothes
- jewellery
- accessories
- general appearance
- mental attitude

This will enable you to determine quickly facts about the person's personality and situation eg:-

- serious
- worried
- happy
- sceptical
- the type of work he does
- his financial situation
- personality

The system of approach is based on the fact that all of us have four major interests in life:-

- our self
- someone else
- our possessions
- our ambitions

A few leading questions will determine which particular ones the person is most interested at this time. From this point a trial approach is made in one or more of the following likely directions.

That is:

You tell the person he is "anxious to know about your.....
isn't that true?" or " You are not quite satisfied with conditions
in your ...."

A slight inflection of the voice, a questioning tone, usually
gets reaction in affirmative or negative. This indicates that
you should follow through with more detail along that line, or
cover up (as later described).

Subjects of Interest

HEALTH
- their own
- someone else
- accident
(person wants peace of mind)

LOVE
- uncertain about someone
- rivals
- quarrels
- untrue
(person wants happiness)

HOME LIFE
- the mate
- children
- relatives
- finances
- friends

- conditions

(person wants security)

BUSINESS
- an employee
- employer
- working conditions
- business prospects
- future
- finances
- relations with others
- new undertaking
- change

(person wants success)

AVOCATIONS
- a sport
- a hobby
- a sideline
- for fun
- money
- pleasure
- relaxation

(person wants friends and popularity)

PUBLIC LIFE
- politics
- social work
- business association
- legal affairs

(person wants fame, honour, etc.)

SOMETHING LOST
- personal article
- money
- valuables
- a friend or relative

(person wants recovery)

TRAVEL
- for pleasure
- business
- education
- by boat, plane or car

(person wants opportunity)

Always give a cheerful and encouraging message. It can readily be seen, that once the line of interest has been established, it is easy to note reactions and follow through with more and more definite details. You must continually be telling something with occasional hesitations, and getting acknowledgements, as the person applies your remarks to his own life.

Whenever you sense a denial, by the person's word or action, these are methods of covering up a false lead:-

1. Qualify your remarks by diverting it to someone near to the person.
2. Change your remark to a prediction, "Even though you cannot see the connection at this time, it will be clear to you in due course. Mark my words!"

The following are sure predictions for anyone:-

- A LETTER within the next few days seemingly unimportant, better look into this carefully though, it means something to you.
- A LUCKY INFLUENCE coming your way, deserved by your past efforts.
- A SUDDEN TRIP in the offing. You know nothing about it now, but certain influences are at work about you, etc.
- A NEW ACQUAINTANCE coming into your life. You will make valuable contacts through this person; to change your entire life.
- BEWARE OF INSINCERE FRIENDS. You are surrounded by a lot of fair-weather people, who talk behind your back.
- BAD ADVICE, watch out for it. People are trying to counsel you unwisely. Don't depend upon others, use your own judgement.
- YOU WILL HEAR FROM SOMEONE, very unexpectedly. Someone you haven't seen for a long while.

ADDENDA

The Drop-turnover Sleight for Cards

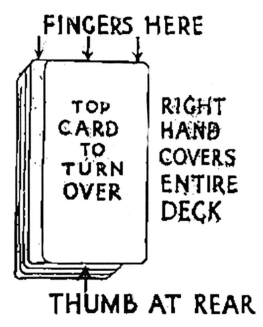

FINGERS HERE

TOP CARD TO TURN OVER

RIGHT HAND COVERS ENTIRE DECK

THUMB AT REAR

The card to be disclosed is on top of pack, in the left hand. Right hand comes over to take the pack from above; fingers grasping the upper edge of the cards and thumb at lower edge.

Palm of right hand thus covers the deck, left thumb simultaneously pushes the top card, off-side (to the right) about half an inch, as shown in illustration.

The deck is dropped from right hand to table, from a distance of about fifteen inches, (best found by trial).

The top card will turn over face up, on top of pack, due to air pressure as the deck falls.

The effect is beautiful, and appears as if this certain card popped right out of the deck, and turned itself face up.

Cards Fly out of the Hat

The card, or cards, intended to "fly" are on top of the deck. Use any soft felt hat with a crease through the crown lengthwise (as they usually are). As you place the pack into hat, the desired cards are thumbed off into one side while the remainder of deck goes into the compartment on the other, side of the centre ridge (unknown to the audience, of course.

It must appear as if you simply placed the pack in the hat. Left hand is holding the hat by the crown from the outside, and gives a little squeeze so that the card(s) in compartment "A" stand upright on edge. Right hand now takes hold of the hat by the brim, while with left thumb and finger you snap sharply on the crown of the hat at a point directly beneath where the separate card(s) rests. This causes same to fly up and out of the hat in a surprising and effective manner.

(This method may also be used as a means of forcing one or several desired cards)

"X-ING THE CUT—(A SUBTLE CARD SLEIGHT)

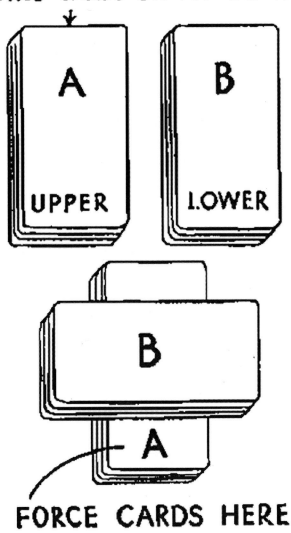

63

The card, or cards, you desire to force are on top of the deck. Have someone cut the deck into two packets.

As soon as this is done, you place the lower portion on top of the upper, only crosswise (as illustrated), thus "marking the cut".

As a bit of misdirection, remark that -

"You have not been influenced in any way... you cut wherever you pleased?"

(This takes their minds off whatever has actually happened.)

Now tell the party to -

"Remove the upper packet and look at the card you cut to"... indicating the top card of lower packet.

This actually forces the original top card of the pack, though no one ever suspects it. It seems so fair and clean-cut that it fools those who know about ordinary methods of forcing.

The End

GLOSSARY OF TERMS

A

Absent Healing
Healing that takes place when the healer is not in direct contact with the person to be healed.

Absent Sitter
A person, not present during a sitting, on whose behalf readings are given..

Acupuncture
Traditional Chinese medical practice that involves sticking needles into specific locations on the body. See also healing.

Agent
(a) Person who attempts to communicate information to another in an ESP experiment. Cf. percipient.
(b) The subject in a psycho kinesis experiment.
(c) Person who is the focus of poltergeist activity.

Akashic Records
"Memories" of all experiences since the beginning of time, believed by some mystical doctrines to be stored

permanently in a spiritual substance (Akasha).

Alien Abduction Experience

Reported experiences of being abducted by alien creatures, often into spacecraft. Abductees often experience lost time and suffer loss of memory. When memories are recovered, often using hypnotic regression, abductees may report that surgical operations were performed on them. See also temporal lobe activity.

Alpha Rhythm

Electrical activity in the brain (about 10 cycles per second) associated with a state of mental relaxation. See also EEG.

Altered State of Consciousness (ASC)

A term used to refer to any state of consciousness that is different from "normal" states of waking or sleeping. ASCs include hypnosis, trance, ecstasy, psychedelic and meditative experience. ASCs do not necessarily have paranormal features.

Ancestor Worship

Religious practices involving the veneration of dead ancestors.

Angels

Benevolent spiritual beings who help people in need. See also guardian angel.

Animal Magnetism

A term coined by F.A. Mesmer to refer to a putative force or fluid capable of being transmitted from one person to another, producing healing effects. See also Mesmerism.

Animal Mutilation

Refers to cases in which animal corpses (often cattle) have been found with bizarre injuries that do not seem to have a normal explanation in terms of illness, accident or action of predators. Cuts and injuries often appear to have been carried out with surgical precision. Typically the corpse is drained of blood. Certain body parts may be absent (e.g., genitals).

Animal Psi
Paranormal abilities exhibited by animals. Also known as "Anpsi".

Animism
Religious practices based on the belief that all living things and natural objects have their individual spiritual essence or soul.

Announcing Dream
A dream believed to announce an individual's rebirth. See also reincarnation.

Anomalous Experience
A general term referring to unusual experiences that cannot be explained in terms of current scientific knowledge. Cf. psi.

Anomalous Phenomena
Natural phenomena that cannot be explained in terms of current scientific knowledge. See also Fortean phenomena.

Anoxia
See cerebral anoxia.

Anpsi
See Animal Psi

Apparition
A visual appearance (cf. hallucination), often of a person or scene, generally experienced in a waking or hypnagogic / hypnopompic state. See also crisis apparition, ghost, haunting.

Apport
A physical object which appears in a way that cannot be explained (seeming to come from nowhere). Apports are often

associated with the seance room and physical mediumship. Cf. deport. See also materialization, teleportation.

Artefact

In parapsychology, false evidence of paranormal phenomena, due to some extraneous normal influence.

ASC

See altered state of consciousness.

Astral Body

A term used by occultists, spiritualists and theosophists to refer to a supposed "double" of the person's physical body. The astral body is believed to be separable from the physical body during astral projection (out of body experience) and at death. See also Ka.

Astral Projection

A term used by occultists, spiritualists and theosophists for the out of body experience. It is believed to result when the astral body separates from the physical body.

Astrology

A theory and practice which attempts to identify the ways in which astronomical events are correlated with events on earth (e.g., with an individual's personality and biography, or with social and political trends).

Atavism

Re-emergence of ancestral characteristics; a genetic throwback.

Augury

Divination.

Aura

A field of energy believed by some to surround living creatures. Certain clairvoyants claim to be able to see the aura (generally as a luminous, coloured halo). See also Kirlian photography.

Automatic Art

See automatism.

Automatic Writing

The ability to write intelligible messages without conscious control or knowledge of what is being written. See also automatism, dissociation.

Automatism

Physical activites (e.g., arm movements, writing, drawing, musical performance) that occur without the automatist's conscious control or knowledge. Also known as motor automatism. See also automatic writing, dissociation.

Autoscopy

(a) Seeing one's "double". See also astral body.

(b) Looking back at one's own body from a position outside of the body. See also out of body experience.

B

Ba

Ancient Egyptian concept of a person's essence, believed to be be immortal. Cf. Ka. See also Soul.

Banshee

In Gaelic belief, a female entity who heralds a death by groaning and screaming.

Bardo

In Tibetan Buddhism, an intermediate state of existence, usually referring to the state between life and rebirth.

Basic Technique

Term used in card-guessing tests of clairvoyance, in which the top card of the deck is placed to one side after each guess.

Billet Reading

Procedure in which a question is secretly written on a piece of paper which is folded or sealed in an envelope, and handed to the psychic who attempts to answer the question. Various trickery can be employed by fraudulent psychics and mentalists.

Bilocation

Being (or appearing to be) in two different places at the same time. See also autoscopy.

Biofeedback

A general term for techniques that involve giving a person information about their current physiological state (e.g., heart rate, EEG). Biofeedback is used to enable people to control consciously their physiological processes.

Bio-PK

Psychokinetic effects on biological processes. See also DMILS.

Black Art

Conjuring technique of concealing objects using black covers against a black background. Also used by fraudulent mediums.

Black Magic

Magical spells or rituals practiced with the intention of harming others. Cf. white magic .

Blind

An experimental control in which subjects are not informed of certain key features of the experiment. Also used to refer to a procedure where a judge is asked to compare targets and responses without knowing which responses were made to which targets. See also double blind.

Blind Matching (BM)

An identical procedure to open matching, except that the key cards are unseen by the subject.

Book Test

(a) A communication in which the sitter is asked to look at

a specific book and page in order to receive a significant message.

(b) An effect in which the psychic or mentalist divines the words written on a particular page of a book.

C

Cabinet
A box or curtained enclosure in which a physical medium is secured and from which various phenomena may manifest (e.g., lights, objects moving, instruments played). Certain stage magicians can simulate this procedure with great effect.

Call
Response made by a subject in a card-guessing or other ESP test.

Candomble
A Brazilian spiritist religion. See also Umbanda, Voodoo.

Card Guessing
An experimental test for ESP in which subjects guess the identity of a set of cards (e.g., playing cards or Zener cards).

Cartomancy
Fortune telling using cards. See also tarot.

Cerebral Anoxia
Lack of oxygen to the brain, often causing sensory distortions and hallucinations. Sometimes used to explain features of the near-death experience.

Chance
Random, unpredictable influences on events.

Channeling
Receiving messages and inspiration from discarnate entities. See also medium.

Charm
A spell or object possessing magic power.

Christian Science
A religious healing movement founded by Mary Baker Eddy. Rejects orthodox medical practice.

Cipher Test
A coded message left by a person who intends to communicate the cipher after death.

Circle
A group of people who hold seances. See also mediumship.

Clairaudience
The paranormal obtaining of information by hearing sounds or voices. See also clairvoyance, clairsentience.

Clairsentience
An archaic term that refers to the paranormal obtaining of information using faculties other than vision or hearing. Cf. clairaudience, clairvoyance, empathy, intuition.

Clairvoyance
A general term that refers to the paranormal obtaining of information about an object or event. In modern usage, this does not necessarily refer to obtaining information visually. Cf. clairaudience, clairsentience, ESP, psi.

Clairvoyant
See clairvoyant medium.

Clairvoyant Medium
Or clairvoyant. A person who obtains information paranormally (often by spirit communication) without the need to enter into a trance state. Cf. trance medium.

Closed Deck
A set of cards used in a card-guessing test where each card appears a fixed number of times. Statistical analysis of research data using a closed deck differs from statistical analysis of data using an open deck.

Coincidence

The occurrence, within a short space of time, of two or more meaningfully related events and without any apparent causal connection between them. Coincidences are sometimes bizarre and extraordinarily improbable. See also synchronicity.

Cold Reading

A reading given with no prior knowledge of the sitter. Often a mixture of very general statements which could apply to anyone, together with inferences made from cues presented by the sitter (e.g., physical appearance, clothes, tone of voice, statements made). Cf. hot reading.

Collective Apparition

An apparition seen simultaneously by more than one person.

Collective Unconscious

Concept put forward by C.G. Jung to refer to a level of unconscious thought and experience shared collectively by humans.

Communication

In mediumship, a message purported to be from a discarnate entity.

Communicator

A discarnate entity from whom the medium receives messages. See also drop-in communicator.

Confederate

A person who secretly provides information to a fraudulent psychic or mentalist.

Conjuring

Using trickery to simulate paranormal effects, generally for the purpose of entertainment.

Contact Mind Reading

A technique simulating telepathy, in which the "mind

reader" (who generally holds a hand or arm) responds to slight muscle movements produced unconsciously by the person whose mind is apparently being read. Also known as muscle reading, Cumberlandism or Hellstromism.

Control

(a) In experimental parapsychology a procedure undertaken in order to ensure that the experiment is conducted in a standard fashion and so that results are not unduly influenced by extraneous factors. See also control group, artefact.

(b) In spiritualism, a discarnate entity who communicates with a trance medium and who generally controls the trance state.

Control Group

A group of people whose performance is compared with that of experimental subjects. Cf. experimental group.

Corn Circle

Circular (or more elaborate) formations found in growing crops, most commonly in Southern Britain. Sometimes they are associated with UFO sightings. Many formations appear to have been intelligently created and to have some symbolic meaning. Despite several "confessions" made by various individuals and groups, the crop circle mystery remains unsolved.

Correlation

An association between two or more events or variables.

Correlation Coefficient

A mathematical index of the degree of association between two or more measures.

Cosmic Consciousness

A blissful experience in which the person becomes aware of the whole universe as a living being. See also altered state of consciousness, mystical experience.

Coven

A group of witches

Crisis Apparition

An apparition in which a person is seen within a few hours of an important crisis such as death, accident or sudden illness.

Cross-correspondence

(a) Separate items of information, received independently by two or more mediums, which make sense only when pieced together.

(b) THE cross-correspondences is a classic case of highly complex cross-correspondences which continued from 1901 to 1932 among a group of automatists associated with the Society for Psychical Research.

Cryptomnesia

Knowledge (acquired in normal ways) that may be revealed without the person remembering its source. Such memories may falsely appear to be paranormal revelations. Sometimes cryptomnesia is used as an explanation for apparently paranormal experiences such as xenoglossy or past-life memories.

Crystal Gazing

Staring into a reflecting surface (e.g., mirror, glass, crystal, liquid) in order to obtain paranormal information. Also known as scrying. See also divination.

Cumberlandism

See contact mind reading.

Curse

Words spoken or written in order to influence others paranormally, causing them harm. See also spell, hex.

D

Daemon (Daimon)

A guardian spirit who communicates inspiration and advice. See also guardian angel.

Death

Generally understood to be the extinction of an organism's life. Many doctrines assert some form of mental or spiritual survival of physical death. See also deathbed experience, haunting, mediumship, near-death experience, reincarnation.

Deathbed Experience

A dying person's awareness of the presence of dead friends or relatives. See also near-death experience.

Decline Effect

A decrease in performance on a psi test when the test is repeated. Cf. incline effect.

Deja Experience

See deja vu.

Deja Vu

A person's feeling that current events have been experienced before.

Delta

A term used to refer to any kind of anomalous experience.

Dematerialization

The paranormal fading or disappearance of a physical object. See also deport.

Demonic Possession

Possession by evil spirits. See also exorcism.

Deport

The paranormal movement of objects out of a secure enclosed space. Cf. apport. See also dematerialization, teleportation.

Dice Test

Experimental techniques for investigating psychokinesis, in which a subject attempts to influence the fall of dice.

Direct Voice

A voice heard in a seance which does not seem to emanate from any person. The voice may seem to come out of thin air, or from a trumpet used specifically for this purpose. Cf. indirect voice.

Discarnate Entity

A spirit or non-material entity. Often used to refer to the personality of a deceased individual. See also channeling, communication, mediumship, possession, survival.

Displacement

Responses on a psi test that correspond systematically to targets other than the intended one (e.g., those before or after).

Dissociation

Activity performed outside of normal conscious awareness, or mental processes that suggest the existence of separate centres of consciousness.

Divination

Practices involving the interpretation of signs or symbols that seek to obtain oracular knowledge of events. Examples of divinatory practices are geomancy, tarot, I Ching, sortilege, and reading tea leaves.

Divining Rod

A forked rod (or sometimes a pair of L-shaped rods) used in dowsing.

DMILS

"Direct Mental Interaction with Living Systems". Psychokinetic influences on physiological processes. See also Bio-PK.

Doppelganger

A mirror image or double of a person. See also astral body.

Double

A duplicate of one's own body. See also astral body

Double Blind

An experimental procedure in which neither the subject nor experimenter is aware of key features of the experiment.

Down Through Technique (DT)

An experimental test for clairvoyance in which the person guesses the order of a stacked series of target symbols (e.g., cards) from top to bottom. Cf. up through technique.

Dowsing

The paranormal detection of underground water or mineral deposits (or lost persons and objects) using a divining rod or pendulum.

Dream

See paranormal dream.

Drop-in Communicator

An uninvited communicator who 'drops in' at a sitting.

E

Earthquake Effect

A phenomenon produced by the physical medium D.D. Home, involving the room shaking as if there was an earthquake.

Ecstasy

An altered state of consciousness in which the person experiences great rapture and loss of self-control. Cf. trance.

Ectoplasm

A semi-fluid substance exuded by a physical medium from which materializations may form.

EEG (Electro-encephalography)

A method of recording variations of electrical activity in the cortex of the brain.

Electronic Voice Phenomena (EVP)

See Raudive voices.

Elemental Spirit

A spirit associated with one of the classical four elements (fire, earth, air and water). See also animism.

Elongation

Paranormal extension of the physical body, reported in some mystics and physical mediums.

Empath

Someone who shows considerable empathy, especially of the apparently psychic type.

Empathy

The ability to understand the experience or emotional state of another person or animal. Often used to refer to an apparently psychic ability to experience another person's sensations, pain or emotions. Cf. clairsentience, intuition.

Entity

See discarnate entity.

ESP

See Extrasensory Perception.

ESP Cards

See Zener Cards.

Etheric Body

Similar to astral body.

Evil Eye

Alleged ability of some people to harm others by looking at them.

EVP

Electronic Voice Phenomena. See Raudive voices.

Evocation

The summoning of (often evil) spirits using a magical

incantation or ritual. Cf. invocation.

Exorcism

A religious or quasi-religious rite to drive out evil spirits. See also possession.

Experiment

A test carried out under controlled conditions.

Experimental Group

A group of subjects who undergo a specific experimental procedure. Often results from this group are compared with those of a control group.

Experimental Parapsychology

Parapsychological research involving experimental methods rather than survey techniques or the investigation of spontaneous cases.

Experimenter

The person who conducts the experiment.

Experimenter Effect

Influence that the experimenter's personality or behaviour may have on the results of an experiment.

Extradimensional

Originating outside our normal space-time reality. Cf. extraterrestrial.

Extrasensory Perception (ESP)

Paranormal acquisition of information. Includes clairvoyance, telepathy and precognition. See also psi.

Extraterrestrial

Originating beyond planet Earth. Not normally considered to be extradimensional.

F

Fairy

Small, human-like mythical being. May be benevolent or malevolent.

Faith Healing
Healing that is associated with prayer or belief in Divine power.

False Awakening
An experience in which a person believes he or she has woken up, but actually is still dreaming.

Faraday Cage
A wire mesh enclosure that provides a shield to radio waves.

Feedback
The giving of information to subjects about their performance on a test. See also biofeedback.

Fire Walking
Walking on red-hot coals, without pain or damage to the feet.

Flying Saucer
A term, coined in 1947, to refer to unknown disk-like aerial objects, often believed to be extraterrestrial spacecraft. The term has now been largely superseded by "UFO".

Focal Person
Person who is at the centre of poltergeist activity.

Forced-Choice Test
An ESP test in which the subject guesses from a predetermined list of alternative targets.

Fortean Phenomena
Strange phenomena, especially those which challenge conventional scientific knowledge. Named after the American researcher and writer Charles Fort. Fortean phenomena include those generally considered paranormal, but also bizarre non-paranormal events such as monsters and prodigies, extraordinary coincidences, and unusual rains.

Fortune Telling
Various practices which aim to divine future events. See

also divination.

Fraud

The deliberate faking of paranormal phenomenena, generally for the purpose of financial gain, psychological manipulation, or notoriety. Faking for the purpose of entertainment (e.g., by stage magicians and mentalists) is not normally classed as fraud.

Free-Response Test

An ESP test in which the subject responds freely (does not choose from a fixed list of targets). For example, the subject may write down or draw their impressions, or may talk freely into a tape recorder. In order to assess the accuracy of the responses, they are compared with various targets (including the actual target) by a judge. See also preferential matching.

G

Ganzfeld

A technique for investigating ESP in which the person experiences an absence of patterned stimulation. This generally involves the subject wearing halved table-tennis balls over the eyes while listening to hiss (white noise) through headphones.

General Extrasensory Perception (GESP)

ESP in which it is unclear whether the results are due to clairvoyance, telepathy, precognition or retrocognition.

Geomancy

A system of divination involving the interpretation of lines or figures.

GESP

See general extrasensory perception

Ghost

Popular term for an experience believed to indicate the

presence of the spirit of a deceased person. See also apparition, haunting, poltergeist.

Gimmick

In conjuring, any small concealed apparatus that is used to produce a magical effect. Also used by fraudulent mediums.

Glossolalia

Unintelligible speech generally uttered in a dissociated or trance state. Also known as "speaking in tongues". See also xenoglossy.

"Goat"

Name given to a subject in a psi test who does not believe in the phenomenon. See also "sheep", sheep-goat effect.

Guardian Angel

An angel believed to protect the individual. See also guide.

Guide

A spirit who is believed to assist a person's spiritual journey. See also angel, guardian angel

H

Hallucination

A sensory experience that does not correspond to physical reality. See also apparition.

Haunting

Paranormal phenomena such as apparitions, unexplained sounds, smells or other sensations that are associated over a lengthy period of time with a specific location. Cf. poltergeist.

Healer

Someone who claims the power of healing.

Healing

Generally indicates cures that cannot be explained in terms of accepted medical principles. See also faith healing, psychic healing, spirit cures.

Hellstromism
See contact mind reading.

Hex
(a) An evil spell or magical curse.
(b) To practice witchcraft.

Hit
A response that accurately matches the target. Cf. miss.

Hot Reading
A reading given in which prior knowledge of the sitter has been obtained, often using devious or fraudulent means. Cf. cold reading.

Huna
An Hawaiian religious practice involving clairvoyance, precognition, healing, miracles and magic.

Hyperacuity
See hyperaesthesia.

Hyperaesthesia
Exceptionally acute sensory awareness.

Hypnagogic Imagery
Imagery occurring in the hypnagogic state (occuring while dropping off to sleep).

Hypnopompic Imagery
Imagery occurring in the hypnopompic state (occurring while waking up).

Hypnosis
An ASC involving a heightened degree of suggestibility. See also Mesmerism.

Hypnotism
See hypnosis.

I

I Ching
Ancient Chinese "Book of Changes". It describes 64

hexagrams (patterns of 6 broken and unbroken lines) which are used in a divinatory practice involving the throwing of yarrow stalks or coins.

Illusion

(a) An appearance that leads the person to draw mistaken conclusions.

(b) In conjuring, a perceptual trick.

Imagery

The ability to perceive images in the mind. These may be visual, auditory, tactile, etc.

Immortality

Various beliefs based on the assumption that some aspect of personal existence survives death.

Incline Effect

An increase in performance on a psi test when the test is repeated. Cf. decline effect.

Incorruptibility

Inexplicable lack of decay in a corpse.

Indirect Voice

Mediumistic phenomenon in which the discarnate entity appears to speak using the vocal apparatus of the medium. Often the voice will sound very different from the medium's normal voice. Cf. direct voice.

Instrumental Transcommunication

Use of recording equipment to produce evidence interpreted as communication from deceased persons or other entitites. See also. Raudive voices, pareidolia.

Intuition

The non-paranormal ability to grasp the elements of a situation or to draw conclusions about complex events in ways that go beyond a purely rational or intellectual analysis. Cf. clairsentience, empathy.

Invocation
Summoning benevolent spiritual beings. Cf. evocation.
ITC
See instrumental transcommunication.

J

Judge
Person who compares targets and responses in an psi experiment.

K

Ka
Ancient Egyptian term for the double or astral body. See also Ba.
Karma
Hindu and Buddhist ethical doctrine of "as one sows, so shall one reap". See also reincarnation.
Key Cards
Reference cards used to indicate each target alternative in a card-guessing test.
Kirlian Photography
A photographic method involving high frequency electric current, discovered by S.D. & V. Kirlian in the Soviet Union. Kirlian photographs often show coloured halos or "auras" surrounding objects.
Kundalini
In Yogic belief, a source of tremendous vital energy that may be stimulated by various practices. Kundalini, or the "Serpent Power", is believed to provide energy for paranormal phenomena.

L

Laying on of Hands
A healing practice, in which the healer's hands are placed

on or near the body of the sick person.

Levitation

The paranormal raising or suspension of an object or person.

Life after Death

See survival.

Life Review

Flashback memories of the whole of a person's life, often associated with the near-death experience.

Lucid Dreaming

Dreaming in which the person is aware that the experience is a dream. Often associated with feelings of aliveness and freedom, and with the ability to control dream events.

Lucidity

(a) An early term for clairvoyance.

(b) Lucid dreaming.

Luminous Phenomena

The experience of strange lights or glows, often around objects or people. See also aura.

Lycanthropy

The supposed magical transformation of a person into the form of a wolf. See also shape-shifting, therianthropy, werewolf.

M

Macro-PK

Psychokinetic effects that can be directly observed rather than only inferred from statistical analysis. Cf. micro-PK.

Magic

(a) Practices that aim to use paranormal or spiritual means to influence events. See also white magic, black magic.

(b) The art of conjuring.

Magician

A person who practices magic.

Majority Vote Technique

An ESP procedure in which several subjects guess a target (or one subject makes several guesses). The most frequent guess is used as the response.

Mantra

A sacred sound or sacred syllables used in meditation. See also transcendental meditation.

Match

An alternative term for hit.

Matching

See preferential matching, matching tests.

Matching Tests

Card guessing tests in which the subject uses key cards when making guesses. See also blind matching, open matching, screen touch matching.

Materialization

The formation of a visible and tangible object or human shape during a seance. Cf. apport.

Mean Chance Expectation (MCE)

The most likely chance score in a psi test.

Medicine Man / Medicine Woman

A witchdoctor or shaman.

Meditation

Mental or physical-mental techniques which aim to produce spiritually desirable states of consciousness. See also ASC, Yoga.

Medium

A person believed to act as an intermediary between discarnate entities and the living. See also clairvoyant medium, trance medium, mental mediumship, physical mediumship.

Mediumship
Activity of a medium.
Mentalism
A branch of conjuring involving the simulation of psi.
Mental Mediumship
The paranormal obtaining of information by a medium. Cf.
physical mediumship.
Mesmerism
A system of healing developed by F.A. Mesmer, involving
the induction of trance states and the supposed transfer
of animal magnetism. People in Mesmeric trance often
showed paranormal abilities such as clairvoyance.
Message
See communication.
Metal Bending
Psychokinetic ability to bend metal objects. A phenomenon
popularised by Uri Geller.
Metamorphosis
See shape-shifting.
Metempsychosis
Another term for reincarnation.
Micro-PK
Psychokinetic effects that cannot be directly observed,
but only inferred from the statistical analysis of data. Cf.
macro-PK.
Mind Reading
See telepathy.
Miracle
A beneficial event attributed to supernatural or divine
intervention.
Misdirection
Techniques used by conjurers and mentalists to distract a

person's attention or confuse their thinking.

Miss

A mismatch between the target and response. Cf. hit.

Mnemonist

A person who has learned techniques that enable extraordinary feats of memory.

Morphic Resonance

A term coined by Rupert Sheldrake to refer to the way in which the "morphogenetic field" (underlying form) of an object or organism may influence distant fields.

Motor Automatism

See Automatism

Multiple Personality

A psychiatric condition in which the person manifests two or more distinct and separate personalities at different times. Cf. possession.

Muscle Reading

See contact mind reading.

Mystic

(a) A person who has mystical experiences.

(b) Used loosely to refer to psychics, mediums or romantics.

Mystical Experience

ASCs involving experiences of ecstasy, unity, timelessness, loss of self, divine revelation, etc.

Mysticism

Religious or spiritual doctrines which argue that the human mind or soul can directly experience the divine. See also mystical experience, transpersonal psychology.

N

NDE

See near-death experience.

Near-Death Experience (NDE)
Experiences of people after they have been pronounced clinically dead, or been very close to death. Typical features of the NDE are an OBE, life review, a tunnel experience, light, coming to a boundary (marking death), seeing dead friends and relatives, experiencing a loving or divine presence, and making a choice (or being told) to return. Occasionally NDEs can be frightening and distressing. NDEs often have profound effects on the person's later life. See also cerebral anoxia, survival.

Necromancy
Black magic practices involving communicating with the dead.

Newspaper Test
(a) A communication in which the spirit forecasts an item in a future day's newspaper.
(b) An conjuring effect in which a magician or mentalist predicts a future newspaper item.

Null hypothesis
The hypothesis that experimental results are due to chance.

Numerology
A system of divination involving the interpretation of numbers.

O

OBE
See out of body experience.

Object Reading
See psychometry.

Occam's Razor
The principle that we should always prefer the simplest explanation of events.

Occultism

Esoteric systems of belief and practice that assume the existence of mysterious forces and entities.

Omen

A sign that foretells events.

One-Ahead Principle

In mentalism, a procedure for sequentially revealing information where the revealing of one item gives the mentalist the next answer. Also used by fraudulent clairvoyants.

OOBE

See out of body experience.

Open Deck

A series of cards used in a card guessing test where each card is chosen randomly and independently. This enables each target to be selected any number of times. Statistical analysis of research data using an open deck differs from statistical analysis of data using a closed deck.

Open Matching (OM)

A card guessing procedure in which key cards are placed face up on the table. The subject then places the unseen target cards in piles in front of each key card, according to their guesses. See also blind matching.

Oracle

(a) An answer to a question, believed to come from the gods.

(b) a shrine at which these answers are given.

Orgone Energy

A term used by Wilhelm Reich to refer to a universal life force, associated with sexuality.

Ouija Board

A board with letters and numbers on which messages are spelled out by unconsciously moving (with the fingers) a glass or planchette. See also automatism.

Out

In conjuring and mentalism, a convincing explanation for an apparent failure, or a convincing alternative ending to an effect that has not worked as planned. Also used by fraudulent clairvoyants and mediums.

Out of Body Experience (OBE, OOBE)

A fully conscious experience in which the person's centre of awareness appears to be outside of the physical body. See also autoscopy, near-death experience.

P

Palmistry

The art of assessing a person's character and forecasting life events by examining features of the hand. See also divination.

Paranormal

Beside or beyond the normal. Inexplicable in terms of our ordinary understanding or current scientific knowledge.

Paranormal Dream

Dreams in which the dream imagery provides paranormal knowledge (e.g., ESP or precognition). See also announcing dream, lucid dreaming.

Parapsychology

Term coined by J.B. Rhine to refer to the experimental and quantitative study of paranormal phenomena. Now generally used instead of "psychical research" to refer to all scientific investigation of the paranormal. Cf. transpersonal psychology.

Pareidolia

Psychological tendency to interpret a random stimulus (especially a sound or visual pattern) as meaningful. See also. instrumental transcommunication, Raudive voices.

Past-Life Memories

Mental images that are believed to be memories of previous lives. See also reincarnation, past-life regression.

Past-Life Regression

A technique of hypnosis involving regressing people to supposed previous lives. See also reincarnation.

Pendulum

An object suspended by a thread. Movements of a pendulum are often used by dowsers to locate objects or answer questions.

Percipient

Person who receives impressions in an ESP test. See also agent, subject.

Phantasm

An apparition.

Phenomenology

An approach to research that aims to describe and clarify a person's own experience and understanding of an event or phenomenon.

Phrenology

The reading of character and mental ability from the shape of a person's skull.

Physical Mediumship

The production of paranormal physical phenomena (lights, sounds, materialization, elongation, levitation, etc.) by a medium. Physical mediumship often (but not always) involves a state of trance. See also mental mediumship.

Picture Drawing

A free-response ESP test in which the subject attempts to draw impressions of the target.

Pilot Study

A preliminary study, generally of modest scale.

PK

See psychokinesis

Placebo

An inactive treatment often given to a control group.

Placement Test

A test for PK in which the subject attempts to influence the place in which dice or other objects land. See also dice test.

Planchette

A small platform on casters generally used with a ouija board. Sometimes used with an attached pencil to produce automatic writing.

Plant Psi

ESP exhibited by plants.

PMIR

See psi-mediated instrumental response.

Pocomania

A Jamaican spiritist religion. See also Voodoo.

Poltergeist

German word meaning "noisy or troublesome spirit". Poltergeist activity may include unexplained noises, movements of objects, outbreaks of fire, floods, pricks or scratches to a person's body. Unlike hauntings, which are associated with specific locations, poltergeists typically focus on a person (the focal person or poltergeist agent) who is often a young child or adolescent. Many physical mediums experienced poltergeist activity in their childhood.

Possession

Refers to cases in which a person's body is apparently taken over by another personality or entity. Cf. multiple personality. See also demonic possession, discarnate entity.

Prayer

A sincere attempt to communicate with a spiritual being or power.

Precognition

The paranormal awareness of future events. See also prediction, premonition, prophecy.

Prediction

A statement that claims to foretell future events. Cf. premonition, precognition, prophecy.

Preexistence

Belief that the personality or soul exists prior to birth. Cf. survival. See also reincarnation.

Preferential Matching

Technique in which a judge ranks a subject's free responses in terms of their similarity to various possible targets.

Premonition

An experience believed to foretell future events. See also prediction, precognition, prophecy.

Presence

A subjective feeling that a person, animal or discarnate entity is present.

Probability

The likelihood that results in a test were due to chance. See also significance.

Process research

Research that aims to investigate factors affecting psi. Cf. proof research.

Proof research

Research that aims to demonstrate the existence of psi. Cf. process research.

Prophecy

(a) A prediction, usually resulting from a sense of spiritual revelation.

(b) The ability to receive prophetic revelations.

Proxy Sitting

A seance in which another person sits in on behalf of the person receiving a communication.

Pseudo-Random Numbers

Numbers generated by an electronic calculator or computer using a complex mathematical algorithm that simulates a random process. Although the numbers generated are essentially unpredictable, they are not strictly random. See also random numbers, random event generator.

Psi

A term used to encompass all paranormal abilities. Includes both ESP and PK abilities.

Psi-Hitting

Significantly better than chance performance on a psi test.

Psi-Mediated Instrumental Response (PMIR)

Theory put forward by Rex Stanford that psi activity is used to serve an organism's needs.

Psi-Missing

Significantly worse than chance performance on a psi test. Psi-missing is also evidence for psi, because a target can only be missed consistently if the person "knows" what it is.

Psyche

Generally refers to the mind.

Psychedelic

Literally "revealing mind". A class of plants and drugs (e.g., peyote, psilocybin, LSD) that can produce florid ASCs.

Psychic

A person who exhibits psi ability (also used as an adjective).

Psychical Research

Term coined in the late 19th century to refer to the scientific study of the paranormal. Now largely superseded by "parapsychology".

Psychic Healing
Forms of healing using psychic powers. See also laying on of hands, psychic surgery.

Psychic Photography
General term used to refer to paranormal photographic images. See also Kirlian photography, spirit photography, thoughtography.

Psychic Surgery
Actual or simulated surgical procedures carried out by healers.

Psychokinesis (PK)
The paranormal influence of the mind on physical events and processes.

Psychometry
Obtaining paranormal knowledge using a physical object as a focus. Also known as object reading.

Pyramid Power
Belief that pyramid shapes can produce paranormal effects.

Q

Qualitative Method
A research method involving the collection of non-quantitative data (e.g., observations, interviews, subjective reports, case studies). Cf. quantitative method.

Quantitative Method
A research method involving the collection and statistical analysis of numerical data. Cf. qualitative method.

R

Radiesthesia
Theories based on the assumption that living organisms emit some kind of radiation or emanation that is capable of being detected using instruments or by dowsing. See also aura, radionics.

Radionics
Use of instruments to detect radiation from living organisms.
See also radiesthesia.

Random
Refers to events that are, in principle, haphazard and
unpredictable. See also chance.

Random Event Generator (REG)
An electronic device which uses a random physical process
(e.g., radioactive decay) to generate random events or
random numbers.

Random Number Generator (RNG)
See random event generator.

Random Numbers
Numbers generated in an unpredictable, haphazard
sequence.

Random Number Tables
A printed table of random numbers, usually made up
of several rows and columns of computer-generated
numbers. To use the table a starting value is chosen by
randomly selecting a row and column (e.g., by throwing
a dice). Successive numbers are then chosen by working
through the table using any previously chosen systematic
rule. Suitable rules might be (1) moving horizontally to the
right, skipping alternate numbers, or (2) moving vertically
down, selecting every fifth number. The selected random
numbers may then be used, for example, to determine
target sequences.

Raps
The name given to unexplained knocking sounds associated
with physical mediumship and poltergeist activity.

Raudive Voices
Intelligible voices recorded on magnetic tape under conditions

of silence or white noise which are heard only when the tape is played. A phenomenon discovered by Konstantin Raudive. See also. instrumental transcommunication, pareidolia.

Reading

Information given by a psychic or medium to a sitter. See also cold reading, hot reading.

Rebirth

In Buddhism, the belief that there is some continuty of mind from one life to the next. Buddhism, however, does not accept the existence of the individual soul and therefore does not view rebirth as the soul's literal re-incarnation. Cf. reincarnation. See also bardo.

Receiver

See percipient.

Recurrent Spontaneous Psychokinesis (RSPK)

A technical term for poltergeist activity.

Regression

(a) a statistical technique that enables predictions to be made from a set of data.

(b) a technique used in hypnosis, involving suggesting to hypnotized persons that they are returning to an earlier time. Sometimes the regression occurs spontaneously, without suggestion. See also past-life regression.

Reincarnation

The belief that some aspect of a person's being (e.g., consciousness, personality, or soul) survives death and can be reborn in a new body at some future date. Reincarnation is often seen as a repeating cycle of death and rebirth in which future lives are influenced by past and present actions through the law of karma. Cf. rebirth.

Remote Viewing (RV)

An ESP procedure in which a percipient attempts to become aware psychically of the experience of an agent who is at a distant, unknown target location.

Response

An action made by a subject in an experiment.

Response Bias

Tendency of a subject to prefer particular responses.

Retroactive Psychokinesis

Paranormal influence that an agent can have on an experiment after it has been completed.

Retrocognition

Paranormal knowledge of past events.

Ritual Magic

Magical activity involving rites and ceremonies.

RSPK

See recurrent spontaneous psychokinesis.

Run

A set of trials in a psi test.

S

Santeria

A Cuban spiritist religion. See also Voodoo.

Sceptic

A person inclined to discount the reality of the paranormal and to be critical of parapsychological research. Generally seeks rational or scientific explanations for the phenomena studied by parapsychologists.

Score

Number of hits obtained by a subject in a psi test.

Scoring

The process of determining a subject's score.

Screen Touch Matching (STM)

A card-guessing procedure in which the subject and

experimenter sit on opposite sides of a screen which has a small gap at the bottom. Key cards are hung on the screen in front of the subject (the faces may be seen or unseen). Underneath each key card is a blank card that can be seen by both subject and experimenter. The experimenter holds the target cards and the subject indicates the guess on each trial by pointing to the corresponding blank card. The experimenter then places the card in a pile on his or her side of the screen in a position corresponding to that of the indicated blank card. See also blind matching, open matching.

Scrying
See crystal gazing.

Seance
A mediumistic session.

Second Sight
Another name for clairvoyance.

Sender
Another name for agent.

Sensitive
Another name for a psychic.

Sensory deprivation
Conditions of greatly restricted sensory input. See also ganzfeld.

Series
A sequence of runs in a psi experiment.

Serpent Power
See Kundalini.

Shaman
A witchdoctor or medicine (wo)man who communicates with spirits while in trance and who has the power of healing. May also show other paranormal abilities.

Shape-Shifting
Paranormal ability to assume the form of another person, an animal or other entity. See also lycanthropy, therianthropy, werewolf.

"Sheep"
Name given to a subject in a psi test who believes in the phenomenon. See also "goat", sheep-goat effect.

Sheep-Goat Effect
Effect, discovered by the parapsychologist Gertrude Schmeidler, in which "sheep" score higher than mean chance expectation (MCE) on psi tests, while "goats" score lower than MCE.

Siddhis
Name given to paranormal powers associated with the practice of Yoga.

Significance
Results of an experiment are said to be statistically significant when they are very unlikely to be due to chance (and hence, in a psi test, are more likely to be due to psi). The chance probability is reported as the "significance level". To be considered significant, the chance probability must generally be less than 1 in 20 (5%, or 0.05).

Simultaneous Dream
A dream whose elements correspond closely with those in the dream of another person.

Sitter
A person who has a session with a medium.

Sitting
A seance.

Sixth sense
Popular term for ESP.

Skeptic

See sceptic.

Slate-Writing

Writing that appears on a slate during a seance. Often produced by fraudulent mediums and mentalists.

Sleep Paralysis

An (often frightening) state of seeming to being awake but unable to move. See also false awakening.

Somnambule

(a) a person who performs physical activity while asleep (e.g., sleep-walking).

(b) a person in a deep hypnotic state.

Sorcery

Black magic

Sortilege

Divination by lots.

Soul

The spiritual element of a person, generally believed to be immortal. See also Ba, spirit, survival.

Space Brothers

Extraterrestrial entities, channeled by some mediums. See also discarnate entity.

Speaking in Tongues

See glossolalia

SPE

See subjective paranormal experience.

Spectre

A ghost or apparition.

Spell

Written or spoken words believed to have magical power.

Spirit

(a) a discarnate entity.

(b) soul

(c) Divine essence.

Spirit Communication

See communication.

Spirit Cure

Healing that is believed to result from the intervention of spirits.

Spiritism

See spiritualism.

Spirit Photography

Photographs of figures or faces, believed by some to be those of deceased persons. These photographs are generally revealed as fraudulent.

Spiritualism (Spiritism)

Religious doctrines that advocate communication betwen the living and the spirits of the dead using a medium as intermediary.

Spontaneous Cases

Paranormal phenomena that occur in everyday life, unsought and unexpected.

Spontaneous Human Combustion (SHC)

Refers to cases in which a badly burned human body has been discovered in circumstances suggesting that the fire originated spontaneously in or on the body of the victim.

Statistics

Mathematical techniques for analysing and interpreting numerical data.

Stigmata

Unexplained markings on a person's body that correspond to the wounds of Christ.

Stimulus

See target.

Subject

A person whose psi ability is being investigated.

Subjective Paranormal Experience (SPE)
Or Subjective Psi Experience. An experience that the person who has it believes to be paranormal.
Subjective Psi Experience (SPE)
See subjective paranormal experience.
Subliminal Perception
Perceiving without conscious awareness.
Super-ESP Hypothesis
The suggestion that people are capable of unlimited ESP. The super-ESP hypothesis is often presented as an alternative to the survival hypothesis in explaining mediumistic phenomena (the medium is believed to obtain information using super-ESP powers and not directly from the spirit of a deceased person).
Supernatural
Paranormal
Survey
A method of data collection that involves interviewing (or giving questionnaires to) a representative and often large group of people.
Survival
The belief that some aspect of the person (e.g., consciousness, mind, personality, soul) lives on after death of the body.
Synchronicity
A term used by C.G. Jung to refer to coincidental events that are meaningfully but not causally connected.

T

Table-Tilting
Mysterious movements of a table, usually occurring in a seance when a group of people place their hands on the

surface of the table. Often the movements are interpreted as spirit communications. Also known as table-turning or table-tipping.

Table-Turning

See table-tilting.

Target

The object or event which the subject attempts to perceive (ESP tests) or influence (PK tests).

Tarot

A special deck of cards (usually 78) used in fortune telling.

Telekinesis

Paranormal movement of objects.

Telepathy

Paranormal awareness of another person's experience (thoughts, feelings, etc.). In practice it is difficult to distinguish between telepathy and clairvoyance. See also ESP.

Teleportation

Paranormal transportation of objects to a distant place. See also apport, deport.

Temporal Lobe Activity

Electrical activity in the temporal lobes of the brain. Often associated with strange sensations, time distortions and hallucinations. Sometimes used as an explanation for seemingly paranormal experiences such as apparitions and alien abduction experiences.

Theosophy

Quasi-religious and philosophical system of the Theosophical Society, founded in 1875 by Madame Blavatsky. Its paranormal claims were controversially and damningly reported upon by the Society for Psychical Research in 1885.

Therianthropy
The supposed ability to change from human to animal form and back. See also lycanthropy, shape-shifting, werewolf.

Theurgy
Magical practices which aim to contact and communicate with the gods.

Thoughtography
Paranormal ability to produce images on photographic film (e.g., by concentrating on a mental image). Most famously demonstrated by Ted Serios. See also psychic photography.

Thought Transference
See telepathy

Trance
A dissociated state of consciousness, generally involving reduced awareness of surroundings and external events.

Trance Medium
A person who enters a state of trance in order to produce mediumistic phenomena.

Transcendental Meditation
A technique of meditation taught by Maharishi Mahesh Yogi, involving the repetition of a sound (mantra).

Transmigration of Souls
See reincarnation.

Transpersonal Psychology
The study of experiences, beliefs and practices that suggest that the sense of self can extend beyond our personal or individual reality. The subject matter of transpersonal psychology overlaps to some extent with parapsychology, but the two disciplines tend to have different approaches and emphases. Parapsychology is primarily concerned to investigate evidence for and against the reality of paranormal phenomena. Transpersonal psychology, on the other hand,

is more interested in investigating the transpersonal significance of such phenomena (i.e., the ways in which they may give people a sense of connectedness with a larger, more universal or spiritual reality). See also mysticism.

Travelling Clairvoyance
(a) An early term for the out of body experience.
(b) Clairvoyance exhibited when a subject travels in imagination to another location.

Trial
In psi tests, a single attempt to demonstrate paranormal ability (e.g., one attempt to guess a card or one attempt to influence the fall of the dice).

Trumpet
A conical tube (often luminous) used in seances to produce direct voice communication.

U

Ufology
The study of UFOs.

Umbanda
A Brazilian spiritist religion. See also Candomble, Voodoo.

Unidentified Flying Object (UFO)
Unexplained sightings of lights or objects in the sky, often taken to be evidence of extraterrestrial visitations.

Up Through Technique
An experimental test for clairvoyance in which the subject guesses the order of a stacked series of target symbols (e.g., cards) from bottom to top. Cf. down through technique.

V

Veridical
Information or experience that is confirmed by facts and events.

Veridical Dream

A dream that corresponds to real events (past, present or future) that are unknown to the dreamer.

Video ITC

See instrumental transcommunication.

Vision

A religious apparition.

Voodoo

A spiritist and ancestor religion, originating in Africa, and now found predominantly in Haiti, Jamaica and Cuba. Magical rites, trance states and possession all play a major role in Voodoo. See also Candomble, Pocomania, Santeria, Umbanda, zombie.

W

Werewolf

A person who has been magically transformed into a wolf or other dangerous beast. See also lycanthropy, therianthropy, shape-shifting.

White Magic

Magical spells or rituals to produce beneficial effects. Cf. black magic.

White Noise

A hiss-like sound, formed by combining all audible frequencies. See also ganzfeld.

Wicca

System of witchcraft, especially as practiced today in western countries.

Witch

Someone who practices witchcraft.

Witchcraft

Folk magic. See also wicca.

Witchdoctor

A medicine wo(man) or shaman.

X

Xenoglossy

The ability to speak or write in a language that has not been learned. See also glossolalia.

Y

Yoga

Religious philosophy originating in India. It advocates the use of physical and psycho-spiritual techniques to lead the person to higher consciousness. See also meditation, siddhis.

Z

Zener Cards

Set of 25 cards (5 each of circle, square, Greek cross, five-pointed star, three wavy lines) designed by the perceptual psychologist Karl Zener for use in card-guessing tests of ESP. Also known as ESP cards.

9 781906 512514